WOMEN &

GIRLS

SURVIVAL

GUIDE: Everything

You Need to Know, But
No One Would Tell You!

by

Vickie Vaughn

Personal and Social Safety Guide (with assessments)
Contains mature subject matter although not graphic

Dedication

This book has been a lifetime in the making. It has been collecting dust in the closet of my life for many years. Herein are many stories that must be told. This book is dedicated to all the women who have been severely, emotionally injured and crippled in life, because of a lack of knowledge. You might ask yourself, why should I read this book? It's not written by a famous celebrity or anyone of notoriety. My answer is that you don't have to be famous to have lived life or claim experience in an area.

I have lived this story and I have seen it unfold in the lives of people I have known. I think that too many people don't understand the importance of an open and honest dialogue with their children or loved ones about relationships.

This book is for those who feel like they have never fit in or belonged any place. It is also for those women who have never found their true soul mate and keep asking GOD, "Lord, why not me?" We WILL go through life without ever finding one true, lasting love or a genuine soul-mate.

Within this book are warnings for women to train up their daughters in the way they might go in life. Consider carefully and wisely whom you decide to give your hearts and ears to. Once you have given away your heart, you have lost a piece of yourself forever. The KJV bible states that , "Evil communications corrupt good manners." In addition it asks, "What communion hath light with darkness?" Seriously consider these words of wisdom as you read. You must consider that every action you take will result in a reaction that will sow positive or negative seeds in your life. Always remember, "*There is none so blind as he who will not see.*"

When I first wrote this book, I thought that bad relationships and abuse persisted in certain socio-economic classes and races, but I found that people are people regardless of status in life. When I was in a women's shelter due to circumstances of life, I met a woman of means. She came in one night to escape the physical abuse of her alcoholic husband. She was very intelligent, had a great job and income. She could easily have made it on her own. She was a take charge type of person. She only stayed for a few nights in the shelter because she wasn't accustomed to that type of environment, but we stayed in touch. Sadly, she returned to her jealous, abusive husband. She felt that one source of his jealousy was her ability to earn more than he did.

It's not a pleasant thing to imagine, but that's the reality of life for many women. Arm yourself, your sisters, daughters and cousins to take precautions to keep themselves safe. Aesop told a parable in "The Fox and the Crow." A wily fox wanted a bit of meat in a crow's beak. But she was too high up for him to reach it. He flattered her with fancy words. When he charmed her into opening her mouth, the meat fell out and the fox ate it. The same can be said of a male who wants something from a female. Sometimes there may be flattery and other times there may be force to gain entry into her life. Once the door is opened, "*the monster in the closet*" may emerge if one is in there. God gave Adam a mate because the companionship of an animal was not sufficient. He provided him a helpmeet and a companion in the form of a wife. This was the beginning of the issues between males and females.

The best way to insure success in relationships is to have a Godly and spiritual foundation for their basis. I wish happiness and joy to everyone who reads this book. It is extremely personal for me and hard to share some of these experiences. But I hope that in doing so, someone will reap a benefit.

TABLE OF CONTENTS

Hope

Hope has built mighty nations and crushed the tender heart.
It's saved families and also ripped many apart.

Hope is like a double-edged sword. It holds two parts together
or steals long awaited reward.

What is hope for you? I'll tell you what it can be—
A life-saving raft on a dark raging sea.

Hope is the foundation of religions and dreams that top the
spires. Hope shores up the depths of our deepest desires.

Hope has given life to battered broken limbs. It's also seen the
demise of chances oh so slim.

Dreams of riches and games of chance. The realization that an
invalid might dance.

Desires to one day be, the belle of the ball. Marry a prince and
end up with it all.

Hope has given life to broken bodes in their beds, limbs
crushed, bodies withered they still hope on ahead.

Surely love will come to fill an empty soul. A hand to hold as
time marches on, both together as we get weak and old.

Hope is inspiration or an enemy of precious time.
What is hope in your life? **This only you can truly define.**

CHAPTER 1 –Women's Faulty Ideas About Men

This booklet will be as direct and to the point as possible, so that not one inch of space is wasted. This information is not meant for the exceptions (*which are few and far*) but to the rules (*the guys that practice deception*). There are some really great, faithful, caring guys out there, but not every one of us is so lucky to find one. Some women or girls seem to attract the wrong kinds of guys for whatever reason. We're not sure what is wrong with us. Let me assure you, that's it's not you all the time. It's just that there are so many heels out there. The bad guys outnumber the good ones. If it is you—we need to find out what kind of energy we're putting out there. Let's begin!

The first myth that women need to get past is that men and women are alike. This very idea has led women to get trapped in the games men like to play. They count on females to think that way in order to take advantage of them.

Men and women are not alike physically or mentally. Let's look at the obvious---outward appearance. Of course our bodies differ externally, because men have more muscle mass than females, therefore they don't have the problem of weight gain as time goes on. The extra muscle mass makes them stronger than we are. The weight issue for women is that they put on more pounds to carry babies. They carry more in their hips and breasts in order to support childbearing. Also as the woman goes through menopause and ages, she gains some extra weight so that her body can make the hormones that she loses because of the change. This difference in strength allows men to help us move furniture, build and lift things that we as women often cannot. More muscle equals less fat for men and the opposite for women! That's why men are more reasonably allowed to fight in wars. Men can overpower us, so we need to be better thinkers than fighters. This is why it is important for females to keep themselves out of situations in which they may have to fend off a male's advances. We will discuss this more in later chapters.

There is an increased incidence of rape and molestation in this country. We can pretend like it doesn't exist, but it's there. Much of it goes unreported because of the shame+ guilt issue. In addition to the fact that this act has been perpetrated by someone who is known and trusted by the family or victim. Therefore, women have to be careful for themselves, but even more vigilant of their innocent girls. Never leave your female child(dren) in the care of even a familiar male if at all possible. Vigilant mothers should not leave their helpless little girls in the care of males because the nurturing nature is not there.

"Although it is usually thought of as a male hormone, women's bodies also make testosterone, but at much lower levels than men's. Testosterone has two different effects on the body: anabolic effects which promote growth and muscle building, and androgenic effects such as deepening of the voice and growth of facial hair." (*www.thebody.com*)

The second difference in men and women is in the thought process. Men are concerned with practicality and basics. Men's bodies produce a hormone called testosterone. Although the male brain is larger in size, this doesn't mean that they are more intelligent or better thinkers. Men are more concerned with right now. (*in the moment*). They're survival oriented. Men's bodies produce a hormone called **testosterone**, which makes them produce more body hair than women.

They have hair on their faces, ears, within their noses and ears and perhaps their backs. These same hormones make men more aggressive and sexual than women. This male hormone influencesthe physiology of the male brain and how he thinks. They make him more primal, survivalist and sexual. As we know, just the sight of an attractive female can turn a male into a hunter. This is where the danger for women lies, if those actions are not guided or tempered by a higher spiritual being like God.

From a young age, as young as one year- males are aware of their sexuality. If they explore and become acquainted with these feelings at too early an age, it can lead to trouble.

Men want to break the bank and spend the money on good times. They want drinks, fast cars, games of chance and socialization. They highly value the opinions and comraderie of other males. Men share fish stories, conquests and challenges more readily with their male peers, than with a mate.

Women tend to stick closer to home and family. They are more guarded in friendships. Women are complex thinkers, meaning they think about the past, present and future and it's consequences. On the other hand, women plan for the future. They want a house, a savings account and a retirement plan. The goal of these things is security. A woman is a forward thinker---planning for the future. Women need to feel a sense of safety and security. Remember the parable of the ant and the grasshopper?

The ant worked all summer and put its food away for winter, while the grasshopper played his fiddle and had a good time. Finish this analogy: The female is to the ant what the male is to the

_____.

Men are simplistic thinkers, they think about the **right now** needs. They may enter into a relationship with a woman to fulfill a temporary need for things like a place to stay or sex---- and not consider how it will affect that woman two months or years from now. A young male I met told me that women take things so seriously. Her heart gets broken and the guy thinks "*Oh, she'll get over it*". They never think that she'll be dealing with the fallout from the hurt years from now.

Women by nature are mentally stronger than men. By this I mean that women can take more mental stress and not buckle. They are resilient in the face of adversity and disappointments, because they use HOPE as a pacifier. When faced with long-term stresses, males tend to become dependent upon alcohol or drugs for stress relief. A woman feels the need to talk things out. These two different halves were made by GOD (male and female) to need and depend upon one another to survive. However, most people are not aware of these differences in our natures. The two halves make a complete whole unit, if they work together. We were designed by GOD to help one another. Hence the term *helpmeet*.

The final area in which men and women differ is emotional needs. A male has a massive EGO and high opinion of self. How he looks in the face of others – is as important as breathing. He needs a lot of positive reinforcement and this has to do with his biology as much as anything. The woman he has can be as much a source of pride as the car he drives. Know why a guy's interested in you. He may be telling his friends how fine you are or how foolish you are. If you're attractive that's a bragging right.

Also if he's able to use you for things he needs, that's another thing they brag about. A woman is willing to accept a man if he can offer her security, whether it be emotional and/or financial. She's more willing to accept the inner person (even if he's not attractive on the outside) if he's a quality individual—it's worth it. He can have one eye and one leg. The inner person is what counts most to a woman. I've told a guy that I dated that what interests me is how big a guy's heart is. If he shows me he cares for me. I think it's that way for most normal women.

I've always felt that everyone wants to be loved and respected, even axe murderers. Perhaps that's why they went ballistic! This knowledge of what a woman desires serves as *bait*, when a male is trying to pursue a female. He behaves as if he has those intents in the beginning of the relationship. That's usually what makes a female fall in love in the first place. This is much like the aforementioned flattery that *the fox* uses to get the meat from the crow.

Women develop feelings for a man when he's kind and caring towards her. When he's concerned about how she feels, when he calls every day, when he remembers the special days, if he's concerned about her being sick, when he works hard and brings home the bacon, when he helps out around the house.

I've observed that when a man really cares about a female---
he'll make sure her needs are met to the best of his ability.

Men and women develop and view intimacy in different
ways. Men can develop feelings (*emotions*) for a woman mainly
based upon the physical aspect of the relationship. This makes
us nearly opposites and it's also a two-edged sword, because
men can separate their *physical desire* from their emotions,
whereas women can't compartmentalize those feelings very
well. A man will start a relationship, with the sole purpose of
fulfilling a physical need. He will be intimate with a woman and
then down the road, drop her and tell her that he doesn't care
for her THAT way (*meaning love her*). I know of a situation just
like this.

He's a worm!

This is the story of a young woman who dated a guy for three
years. He was not interested in her because of love, but ego.
She was a doormat and assuaged his small ego and need for
attention. That was the size of it. She was really a nice girl and
she fell in love with him. They dated for more than
four years. After all of that time, he still developed no true
feelings for her. He was dating other females too. He also got
her and another girl pregnant. When the situation became too
messy, he left town. She's still in love and now has two kids to
raise by herself. Meanwhile this woman is still hoping for and
feeling that there's a deeper connection.

That's why time is a woman's best friend. You'd better wait him
out and see what's happening. If it's shallow—he'll eventually
wander off. Know your worth and that you deserve a guy
who's going to give you as much as he takes away.

"In men, high levels of endogenous testosterone (T) seem to encourage behavior apparently intended to dominate -- to enhance one's status over -- other people. Sometimes dominant behavior is aggressive, its apparent intent being to inflict harm on another person, but often dominance is expressed nonaggressively. The act of competing for dominant status affects male T levels in two ways. First, T rises in the face of a challenge, as if it were an anticipatory response to impending competition. Second, after the competition, T rises in winners and declines in losers. Thus, there is a reciprocity between T and dominance behavior." (Testosterone and Dominance in Men / Abstract/ www.bbsonline.org).

Next, men are simple creatures with large egos. There are few men who are as sensitive about things as women are. Women are concerned with small matters. A prime example of this is when men forget birthdays, anniversaries, Valentine's Day or forget to call when they say they will. I have an adult son. I had moved away and often I'd call and tell him, "*Son you need to call me more.*" and he'd say, "*I meant to mom, but I got really busy.*" Finally, I just gave up! I decided that he'll call me when he wants to. However, when I went through one of the worse crises of my life, my son was my biggest supporter and I felt my only friend. For most fellows , it's "*out of sight--- out of mind.*" To sum it up, don't expect them to remember every little thing. It's not going to happen.

You build yourself up to be let down when you do this. They may be very good at it in the beginning, but as the relationship gets old to them, it may become less important.

The main reason men get to mate with females is because they know how to play the game. The game is to observe and know the actions of your prey. See what kinds of signals they give off and then move in for the kill or conquest. Men have no desire to think or behave like women. Their ultimate desire is to obtain that woman's heart and trust so that they can get the upper hand. Old African hunters believed that if one ate the heart of the enemy, they would obtain the strength and power of that person. In a sense this is true of a conquered female. Once a man has won her heart, the body follows and she submits. It is an extremely difficult process to get over a broken heart. Females be careful who you give your heart to. Once you give it away, you lose the power to think clearly, rationally and objectively about the situation.

CHAPTER 2 Beware – Fatal Types of Men

There are several kinds of men out there that women meet. They are dangerous to females. That's why we have to study a male and his behavior before getting involved. Three main categories are The Misogynist (woman-hater), The Player, and The Rapist.   First, is The Misogynist . These men don't think of themselves as such. They may not even be aware of these negative feelings, but they're there under the surface. These men have an underlying anger toward women and it can be for one or two main reasons.

One of these reasons for the anger and resentment is that the male felt victimized by a woman at some point in his life. The reason could be feelings of abandonment or abuse by a mother-figure. It could also be that they were molested by a female at an early age and harbor anger and resentment towards females. My ex-husband told me that he was molested as a boy by a female babysitter. If they explore and become acquainted with these urges and feelings at an early age, it can lead to trouble. I wondered why he was so aggressive and why he had such a warped viewpoint and anger toward women.

He had been married two times (*I later learned*). I became his third wife. He'd beaten the women he was involved with, including me. I'll share this story with you.

When my ex-husband and I were dating, on one occasion his car had gotten stuck in a mud hole. We had stopped to gas up. He got out and asked me to get behind the steeringwheel and give it some gas while he pushed it out. I did as he asked. The mud sprayed the blue suit he was wearing. When I got out of the car to see why the car wasn't budging, he punched me in the eye so hard, I could see stars. I ran back to the car, where my mom was sitting and told her what had happened. I was 19 years old and immature. I couldn't understand what I had done wrong. He never apologized for it. We finally got the car out of the hole. I felt that at this point I was," In for penny, in for a pound." I should have walked away right then!

"Puttem up!"

A second instance of this man's brutality and abuse came about after we had married. On one particular night he wanted to go out to party---without me and I insisted that I come along. I believe that he wanted to meet someone else and I had put a damper on his plans. We rode with his brother and his girlfriend. We went to a small juke joint in a neighboring town. There wasn't a great deal of conversation or dancing. I sat and listened to the music. I got so bored that I went next door to a small diner to order a hamburger. When I got back, he started quizzing me and asking me who I was talking to and what I had done. We stayed out about an hour more. Then we all headed towards home.

We went to his aunt's house, where he wanted me to get out and stay the night. I told him I didn't want to go in. I wanted to go back to my mother's trailer. I wanted to go home. I guess this raised his (T) level. My confronting him in front of his brother made him lose face. He lunged toward me and began pulling me out of the back seat of the car. Not an easy task in *such a limited space. After extricating me, he drug me by my hair into his aunt's house. I shook him loose and darted into the house on my own volition (boosted by fear)—when he followed me into the back bedroom. His brother followed the "man code", which stated that another man was not to interfere in the affairs of another. Especially when it came to putting a woman in her place. He sat limply by in the car with his girlfriend. I'm not sure what she must have been thinking as they both watched. My spouse came in and forced me down onto the bed in the back room. He straddled me and began punching me in the face. He knocked out one of my front teeth. To this day he won't admit to doing it. Much later in life, he was diagnosed with a serious mental disorder called schizophrenia. This is no attempt to excuse his brute behavior, but this shows how unbalanced he was and probably had been for a long time.*

Earlier, I had dropped a bomb on him, by saying that I was two months pregnant. This knowledge must have fueled the anger of a man who had a new wife, no glowing job prospects and a limited income. While hovering over me on the bed, he punched me dead on in the face at least two or three times. I really couldn't feel the pain right then, because of the fear. He got up and came out of his haze of anger only when his elderly aunt called him to the phone. She had called his mother after he refused to heed her calls to, .Stop beating that girl!. He got up and sauntered into the smoky living room, to take the telephone call. That's how I was able to escape. Had I not had that opportunity to run, he probably would have

beat the kid out of my belly. I silently slid out of the back screen door of the old country house. I slid on the ground under what used to be an old smokehouse. There was enough space for my body to get beneath it. It's amazing what you can do when the survival instinct kicks in. It was a short time before he returned. His face was pressed against the frame of the old screen door, as he peered out into the dark night searching for me. His body was silhouetted by the light flowing from inside the room. He left the doorway and went back to the front of the house. He wasn't sure which direction I had gone off in. I believe he was under the impression that I had ran around towards the front of the house to the road. I could hear his muffled voice speaking to his brother in the car. I knew this was my chance to get away or have to hide under the smokehouse until daylight, and be discovered. This was my chance! I slid from under the tiny building and cut across the field in back of the house. The lights from a neighbor's house weren't far away. My path was through a field full of tall dry stalks. The remains of a corn harvest perhaps? I wasn't sure and I didn't care. Across the field and between the stalks I shot into the middle of the cold country night to the house. I was ever aware that my enemy could be behind me. But, I made it and I got help. It was the home of an elderly couple. I remember The Lawrence Welk show playing on their television set. I called my mother to come and pick me up. It never dawned on me until some time later, that these people were related to a young man that I had known before my ex-husband. He had made overtures towards me. I'd found out that he was the same kind of man. Their son was a woman-beater too.

I was downtown one evening when I saw this guy beat his girlfriend. She was a beautiful girl. She was talking to friends in one of the honkey-tonks. He had driven downtown looking for her. He went inside and pulled her out of the place. I remember him lifting her up off the ground and jamming her up against a chain-link fence out in front. Everyone was looking, but no one dared get involved. She was struggling against him and he lifted her up and shoved her into his old brown and white truck. As she was resisting and kicking to free herself and get out of the truck, he closed the door against her foot. I knew what awaited her when they were both out of town and out of our sight. After all of that, she stayed with him and married him. I asked someone who lived in the town many years later, what had happened to her. I was told that she had cancer. She was traveling to and from Louisiana for treatments. Eventually she lost her battle with cancer. I thought what a life she must have had! She stayed with him, until her death.

This was the southern way in Mississippi. It was part of the culture for men to beat their women. Not all men of course, but I saw a lot of this kind of thing. Many women run towards it, but my way was to run from it. I was determined that this man wasn't going to maim me or kill me. That experience traumatized me a lot. It was the end of the short dreadful marriage. I enlisted in the military to get away from him and small town life. I didn't understand why he would do that. I realized that it was anger and a degree of hatred that motivated him. It sure wasn't love! If a guy is beating on a female, it's not love, it's anger! It came out quite often as we've talked, that he resented his mother for giving him away. He was the oldest and only child of eight that she gave away. He was angry he explained, that he'd endured beatings and "*worked in the hot fields from sunup to sundown like a slave*". This abuse occurred while growing up with the aunt and uncle who raised him. He felt that he had been abandoned by his mother and betrayed. His aunt and uncle came out of slavery. Part of that legacy was brutality, which was passed down to him.

Physical violence was part of the southern Black's life. This was the way that African-Americans were taught and it was a legacy. Plantation Master's used violence as a means for getting things done. As a result, this is part of the reason that Blacks in the South have a tendency toward brutality within interpersonal relationships. One could perpetrate violence on a *loved one*, with little fear of consequence. The ex-husband said that another family in town had wanted to adopt him, but his mother had refused to sign the papers. I think his mother felt it was best for him to be with family.

His mom had gotten pregnant out of wedlock. During the 50's and it was frowned upon for a woman to have a child out of wedlock. She eventually married his father and had more kids, but he never seemed to fault his father for this situation, only his mother. His mother had left him with his aunt and uncle and no explanation or rescue attempt. My ex-husband also revealed that he was raped by a female babysitter. Eventually, after many years of medication, therapy and women who fought him back, he stopped beating women. But he was never able to establish real lasting relationships. He still chases women but he tends to gravitate toward loose women or that don't require much emotional maintenance. But they do want money. He can't relate to females on an empathetic or soulful level. Their main interest in him or any man is money. If he has no money in his pocket, there's no relationship. I think it's easier for him to relate that way.

FACTS ABOUT MEN AND RAPE

"Men get raped by other men and even women. Rapists who rape men are heterosexual 98% of the time. Both homosexual and heterosexual men get raped in all parts of society, not just prison. Males usually share many of the feelings of female sexual assault survivors. They may feel guilty, powerless, concerns regarding their safety, denial, shock and anger (www.//shout-out.org).*"*

I've heard these kinds of accounts about rape from several older men. When men that have been victimized at an early age tend to be highly sexual and have trouble with commitment. They harbor aberrant ideas about women and perpetrate the same acts upon other women that have been done to them. This is why women need to teach their girls to be cautious and not allow themselves to be isolated with males, especially those they don't know. These shameful things are not things men will easily confess, because they deal with the same shame that women do when they've been raped.

Men in general often have a terrible sexual history. But then traumatized there is an even worse track record and chance of a strong commitment. They don't understand the word love because it's been distorted. Their view of intimacy is perverted. A person needs food to live and function. Food like sex, is not something that they can be separated from a full life, but when one becomes a food addict (*e.g. anorexic, bulimic*) it's an area that's out of control. How do you know if a man is a woman hater? I always think that time is a woman's friend. It takes time to observe someone and study their behavior patterns. Our Western culture has done us such a disservice by selling the myth of "*love at first sight*". Everyone seems to have bought into that and it has left a heap of divorce and broken promises in its wake.

In ancient times and in Middle Eastern countries to date, matches were and still are made by families. They were made on the basis of what was good for the family and community. Research was done on the families background to insure a good match. The parents communicated with one another and deals were made. Ones word was to be kept if given.

One benefit of this arrangement is that, others could often sense and see more clearly the character of another. If there was dishonesty or guile in the character of an intended this could be spotted. Today, advice seems to serve as a stimulus for a person to make a bad choice. One excuse is that, "*I'm in love.*" The person in love behaves as if they are enslaved in gilded chains from which they can't break free. Ones emotions become enslave the smitten heart.

Females must pay attention. Notice if his behaviors are those of a "*control freak*". He seems very jealous and wants to know where you are all the time, day

and night. He calls frequently for updates. He gets angry very easily. He will speak about women in negative ways. There's no way or any reason a man should refer to a female as a "b - - - h" or other demeaning name even if she is or is not present. He may or may not be respectful of his mother. That's no sure
indicator. I have known men who loved/treasured their flesh and blood (*daughters and mothers*), but separated these feelings---and disrespected women who were not their blood. Take time to know this person.

Your youth and virtue is extremely valuable!   It shouldn't be wasted on someone who isn't worth it. You're worth taking the time to make good decisions. If you get behind in your life plans, you will pay a heavy price for it.

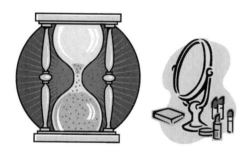

The next type of male that we will look at is "The Player". A well known term, that means a "male tramp". These types of guys get their kicks from seeing how many women they can deceive and collect. They pride themselves on their "*expert game*" and "*swagger*". This alone gives them bragging rights. This next story is about a male who has slept with more than 200 women during his lifetime. He considered himself reformed, but really he's just slowed down. If he wanted a woman, he would go after her with everything he had. He's attractive (*a plus*), he's a very hard worker. He owns his own business. He's generous-- very neat and anally clean. Through observation, I could see that he was a great dad, even to his step children from the various marriages. One major problem was that earlier in his life he'd killed a girl he was dating, because he said that she'd gotten so jealous, she tried to kill him.

He went to jail for a short time. The only reason he got out of the murder charge was because it was her gun and the authorities weren't able to make a strong case against him. He took her gun and turned it on her. He was a man and he was stronger than she was. Couldn't he have easily taken it away from her? I know him, because I met him while on vacation. I was invited to their family gathering and he took a shine to me. He told me that he liked me. I observed him very closely and did some homework. I asked a friend who lived in town what she knew about him. She told me the story of the murder. She also told me that he was dating a younger girl in town who had also gone to jail for murder. She had killed her boyfriend out of jealousy. I thought that they must be kindred spirits. This type of personal violence seemed to be commonplace in the south. I let it go. My friend told me that he was "A Player". This man was seeing the younger

woman and had other women in his life as well. I once
told him that, *"Women must be like a table full or cakes and
candies for you. Lots of treats great to look at and hard to
choose from. When you choose a woman you don't want,
it's like taking a piece of candy, putting it in your mouth
and taking it out. Nobody else wants it after you've
handled it."*

He dated women of different ages and backgrounds. He dated
them for different reasons. He'd been married three times. A
woman who lives with a guy like this has very little self-respect if
she settles for an uncommitted relationship that will more than
likely NOT end in marriage. Players get ego gratification from
this kind of behavior. The longer a woman lives with a guy
out of wedlock the less likely he will marry her, because as
the old saying goes, *"Why buy the cow when you can get
the milk for free?"* You say that now and women don't get
it, but they used to. He eventually ended up *"shacking"*
with the younger girl. However, it didn't work out well
because of his behavior. This man has evaluated each
female and decided how little he would have to invest in
her to get a payoff. Men are going to try to get as much as
they can for as little as they can. They're bargain hunters
of a different sort. Do you think this man loves this girl?
He has no relationship with God, so what's to stop him
from doing anything he likes? And that's just what he did.
He cheated on her with other women. The relationship

didn't last. She took as much from him as she could to hurt him financially. He recovered from it, but she didn't. A woman had to be very strong to accept that she is living with someone who will cheat on her. He has told me that when he is cheating, he will been out all night. He'll tell her that he's working. Everyone works, but very seldom will anyone work all night, even for themselves. I inquired of him, *"If you get home really late , what does she say to you?" He replied, "Nothing"*. He's made it clear, that he doesn't want a jealous woman---and it means you're jealous if you complain about the situation. He told me that he made it a rule, that if he has a woman, she can't have another man, but he can have other women. It sounds outlandish, but he's living the dream. Everything is focused around what he wants, he's self-centered – just like any child. The female he's with is a *"hope-**er**"*. Perhaps she thinks or hopes that she can change him. I know she loves him, she also depends upon him financially. There are a lot of components to any relationship, but is she coming out ahead?

Hope is a double-edged sword. That is what the poem In the beginning of the book refers to. Hope can give you the strength to survive terrible tragedies or it can keep you holding on to a dream or real relationship that may never materialize. It can enable a person to make it through hard times in relationships that may be worth it, but wasting time is also a possibility. So, the *"hope-er"* has to decide which way the blade cuts. Is it in your favor or against you? Why would you wait five or ten years for a guy to marry you or to change his behavior? You might be waiting until he kicks the bucket <u>or</u> you do. Yes, you're supposed to be there for someone if they're sick and need your help. But, I think this special privilege should only apply to someone that you have married and promised your life to. One rule I have if I am dating, is to give a guy a specific amount of time to ask for my hand in marriage. If that isn't the end goal, then what is? Just wasting your time, until the next boat sails in? No thanks, my time (*and youth*) is too valuable to throw away!

The third type of male females should be cautious of is "The Rapist". Many of you might say "DUH! at this one. It's a given, but many women don't know who is or isn't a rapist until they get in a situation that gets out of control. Testosterone which causes men to have more body hair than women, also makes men more aggressive and more sexual than females once they hit puberty. However, as we know there are several causes for rape although it is primarily an act of violence.

A young woman needs to be very careful about the company she keeps. Mass murderers don't present themselves as such, but as nice everyday guys. Most instances of rape among females occur and are perpetrated on them by someone they know. Although it may be frowned up in American society---eastern cultures find it wise to arrange and carefully monitor relationships for females. Modest dress is one component of cultural difference they use to address this issue --- although rape has nothing to do with the way someone is dressed.

Rape is no less rape, even is it is done under the pretense that he "*loves you*". If a man lies to get what he wants from a woman, that's a form of rape. The moral decay of American culture has led to an over saturation and treatment of women in the media as objects of gratification. T.V. images are used by youth who have no moral guidance at home in order to determine how they should present themselves. Women have to be very careful of the company they keep. Don't put yourself in a situation where a man might take physical advantage of you.

Herein is the danger for a woman. If that man is not guided by a higher spiritual being like GOD, he can be destructive for her life.

THE IMPACT OF CULTURE ON RELATIONSHIPS

The idea of romantic-chemical love has hurt women. It is mainly native to the U.S. Romantic love is too fickle to build a foundation for your entire life. Here today, gone tomorrow. Feelings change! Romantic love is based upon physical attraction first, then all else is supposed to follow. Successful relationships are built on mutual goals, values and similarities. In eastern cultures marriages are arranged between families. Families choose the mate for their daughters. This is best because they are able to be more objective about that person. In the past these arrangements were based on alliances and mutual benefit for both families. A man had to bring something to the table in the form of a dowry. He had to show that he had something of substance . In the west, women are left to fend for themselves. Our culture doesn't prepare females for relationships. Therefore, you'd better do your homework and investigate. Although it seems that a person's individual freedom is taken away in the eastern arrangement—look at the mess we're in, in this culture because of too much freedom and choice.

Males have a veritable buffet of women to choose from, because females think so little of themselves. There is an extremely high incidence of date rape, disease, illegitimacy and divorce in America. A remedy for this is to have friends or family help you choose a decent mate. I've asked my friends to help me find a suitable guy to date and they've had as hard a time as I've had finding someone of character. They don't even know of anyone to recommend. That says something about our social state!

Others (friends and family) will know that persons character and I'm sure they won't choose someone shady for you. Get counseling before marriage and ask for advice from people who are mature and successful in their marriages.

Another cultural problem we're facing is that African-American families and females have and still are suffering the effects of the plantation. At one time the role of the Black man was as a stud-breeder. This has been a curse that has carried down until today. Black males mate with females and then leave the family. At one time, this separation was forced upon us, now—it has been inbred and became a voluntary response to so much choice and trifflingness.

I see so many women who lack self-worth and settle for any kind of old trampy man—with a cool line. Some take serious emotional and physical beatings. What I've been through is nothing compared to what I've seen some women endure. I have seen women beaten bloody by brutal men and they keep going back to that never ending cycle. Everyone is begging her to get out and she won't. I keep wondering, "What's wrong with you? Why do you think so little of yourself?" Know what you have to offer the world, a mate and anyone. We often underestimate our own self-worth. Let me tell you this. If you let a man make a fool out of you, he has no sympathy on you. He will use you for as much as you're worth and then go on to the next woman if he is like any of the above mentioned guys. If any young female allows herself to have illegitimate children, she lives on the *"welfare plantation"*. A friend and I were discussing why it was so hard to find a good guy these days. I asked her, *"Why do they (men) always choose the women who aren't doing anything with their lives?"* She said that her boyfriend told her that guys go out and find females who live in the projects *(rent subsidized housing, welfare and food stamps)* to get what they needed from them *(i.e. a place to stay, food, sex, drugs, money)*. When a woman goes out to work every day, she gets tired very quickly of a man sitting on his duff not doing anything. I'm not talking about any one ethnic group or minority. I am speaking of any female who gets caught up before she is self-sufficient.

When the woman on the *"plantation"* gets tired of dealing with the guy because he is abusing her, she puts him out and he moves on to the next woman in the same situation. I'm discussing this issue because our culture has created a self-perpetuating downward trend of females taking care of adult men. This has become especially prevalent among younger females. Women aren't valued, because many of them don't value themselves. If a woman is struggling, the man in her life should help her financially. If a guy cares about you, he'll try to help you financially. I'm not a gold-digger *(but I don't want anybody broke either)*. Even if he doesn't have much, it shows that he's trying to be a man. A wise woman will appreciate the effort he's made to see to her needs. Every little bit helps. You can't say that you love someone and see a need and not acknowledge that by helping out. This should only be happening in a committed relationship. Relationships aren't all about money (I know that!), but you see it's like God's principle of the tithe. Money represents time and commitment. If you share your resources, it's like sharing your time. We spend a lot of our time working.

This is the trend in our culture because many females (young and old) are taking care of a male. That's why the men of today are so weak. Men think a woman is weak if she is generous, giving and open-hearted. If he's a heel, they don't respect her or appreciate her for it. He sees it as an opportunity to take advantage. Let him be the man that God made him to be. They'll appreciate it more.

ASSESSMENT CHAPTER 1 AND 2

1. Name one myth that women have about male/female relationships:_____
_____

2. What is one outward physical difference between the male and female body:

_____
_____

3. A female is most likely concerned with what? S-E-C-
___ ___ ___ ___ ___.

4.What does this saying mean: .Why buy the cow when you can get the milk for free?_____

_____.

5. Name one type of male that a female must be careful of:_____

6. What is a misogynist?_____
_____

7. Name one reason a man resents women:_____

8. Is dominant behavior always aggressive? YES or NO Name one way males show dominant behavior?_____

9. There are several precautions that women can take to choose a mate, name one:

a._____
_____

10. Explain one way our Western culture contributes to the abuse of women?

a._____
_____

11. What's one solution to the problem of abuse?_____
_____
_____

12. Name one problem with the idea of "romantic love":_____
_____.

13. What does the term "welfare plantation" mean?_____
_____
_____.

Chapter 3 - A Woman's Virtue

The value of a woman's virtue can't be understated. The idea of a virtuous woman seems to have lost its steam, but remember the hubbub about Brittany Spears and Jessica Simpson when they announced that they were young women of virtue. People were interested to know more. Was it true? Does she carry herself like a virtuous woman? Will her story hold up? I think deep down inside people are rooting for a return to old fashioned values and lifestyle. Let me share a little story with you. When I was a young girl, I was never told about *"the birds and the bees"*. I remember a 4 or 5 year old boy trying to get me to play doctor with him outside our old shot gun house, but I wouldn't. As early as that the devil was trying to ruin my life. I knew something was wrong with it. I just felt it was wrong.

As I grew into a young teenager, I would watch my older sister. The other kids used to call her "Rootie-Toot-Toot", because she was a wild one. Anything that had action and adventure in it, she was in! She was rebellious, but we didn't know that's what they called it then. I learned a lot from watching her and her friends. I lived vicariously through them. She would never get into the house before her 10:00 curfew. She would hang out on the stoop as they called it in New Orleans. She and her boyfriend would fight, smoke weed, cigarettes, drink wine and sniff cleaning fluid. She also became sexually active at an early age and got herself pregnant at fifteen-years old. She wasn't ready for that kind of responsibility and it was hard for my parents, her and the baby. I would sit and watch all of this going on. I knew this wasn't the life I wanted. No one ever offered me a hit off a "doobie" either.

Once a boy from the neighborhood tried to kiss me. it was a French kiss. I was scared and I had never kissed a boy like that before. I didn't like it! The only thing I knew about were T.V. kisses on the lips. I tried it, but didn't like it. He told my sister and her friends (not in front of me) that I kissed like a fish. From that point on I was scared that some guy would want to kiss me and I couldn't do it right. It scared me away from boys and males for a long time. I was also unattractive and skinny, so nobody was very interested in me. But I always knew that GOD was speaking to my heart to hold out and do the RIGHT thing. My fear of kissing may have been a blessing in disguise. It may have bought me more time to develop myself. When I saw my sister struggling with that baby, that solidified my idea that I was not having sex until I got married and had a husband to help me. Momma didn't want to take care of any more babies.. My parents were not talkers. They barely spoke to each other. They didn't come out and tell us about life. Their parents hadn't told them anything about it either, so we lacked guidance. We were pretty much on our own, however God's voice always told me what was right and wrong. I had high expectations for myself and that voice came from inside.

I was and am by no means a saint, but I wanted a different kind of life for myself. I wanted order and security. The King James bible talks about Dinah and Tamar. They were virtuous women who were (raped) violated. In the case of Dinah (Genesis 34) , a man called Shechem, from a neighboring tribe saw her and wanted her. Dinah was the daughter of bible patriarch, Jacob. Jacob had 12 sons. Obviously, having 12 sons, Jacob must have had other daughters besides Dinah, but Dinah is the only daughter we know about. Shechem invited her family to a party and got them drunk. While thus, he took advantage of her. He took her virtue, but he paid with his life and that of his family. She was of a chosen family. As custom dictated , once a woman lost her virtue and was not married she was an outcast. In the case of Tamar (II Samuel 13), Amnon her half-brother said that he loved her so much he couldn't eat. He asked the advice of a "*friend*" who told him how to trick the girl and take advantage of her. He pretended to be sick and need help.   As Tamar administered aid to him he took advantage of her. Once he had her, his guilty conscience --- would not allow him to look at her. He no longer wanted her. He also refused to marry her. His life was taken by her half-brother as for the deed. These two cases were similar and different in one respect. They were alike because both men went to great lengths to execute and plan their action. They used trickery to gain what they wanted. Neither had no thought of what the consequences could be for themselves and the women they had hurt. Their thought was for immediate gratification.

Both men paid with their lives. However, the difference was that Shechem was willing to do the honorable thing and marry Dinah, because he loved her. He wanted to right the wrong. He knew the law of the land, but he should have considered them before taking the course he did.   His entire family was killed because of his actions.   Amnon also knew the laws of his time and didn't care how it affected Tamar. He had no true love for the girl or he would have waited. As you can see men have been the same across the ages. True love shows patience and respect. Women also be careful not to let men use your caring and nurturing nature to trap and betray you. A female's virtue is a special gift that she can give to one man at one time in her life. It should be given to someone whom she really cares about and who returns that feeling. When a woman allows herself to love a man who doesn't return that love by way of action, it makes her feel worthless and ashamed. This is because it takes something valuable from her. She has lost part of herself. We need to take this seriously. A woman's strength is found in her virtue. Much like the strength that was bound up in Samson's hair. When it was cut, he was weakened. Stay pure and chaste as long as you can! There are too many broken sisters out there (*red, yellow black and white*). I was talking to an African man. I asked him what was the difference between women of his culture and ours. He said, "*A woman is a woman, it doesn't matter what country. They all say the same thing*". The same can be said of men.

Try not to put yourself in a position where you can be taken advantage of. Many women have been raped by men they know. They don't report it because, you know how it goes! The bible clearly shows you that rape or violation of women has gone on from the beginning of time. The loss of so much virtue at such early ages in our society, is tragic and something to be mourned.

There's a sign along the highway I used to travel to work. It advertises "NO RING-NO FLING". It reminds me that a woman's virtue is what gives her respect for herself and it gains the respect of men when they see she's not loose. It also gives her strength, because when a female knows she's pure—it makes her spiritually strong within herself.

Much like Sampson's hair, once it has been shorn, cut or taken, there is a vulnerability and weakness that sets in. When a woman gives herself to a man who doesn't care for her, she feels worthless. She has regrets that she can never erase. After 18 years of saving myself for the right man, do you know how I lost my virtue?

I grew up in a small Mississippi town. We moved there after my parents divorced in the late 1970's. I made my stand clear early on that I was "saving myself for the right fellow". In addition to that, I said that I was considering becoming a nun as an occupation. The local town jesters who stood on the corners all day would see me and call me "The Nun" or "Whitfield" (the name of the state mental institution). I didn't care, that they called me crazy. I used to be in my own universe and it was fine. Yes, it bothered me some, but I always had my own ideas and I knew they were right. I didn't let it get to me. Many of the guys who were interested in me would come to my grandmother's house to sit and talk to me (courting) of the old fashioned type. They were scared of me because I think they could sense I was nervous. They would soon get tired of just hanging around me and not come back. I guess because we weren't seemingly getting any where. I felt like it was okay because I hadn't lost anything, SO WHAT!. Many times my sister and I would go riding and out to eat with some of the guys whom we considered just friends. She'd smoke weed and talk trash. We'd go and park out by the lake—and there wasn't any hanky-panky. We'd all talk, have fun and listen to music.

The guys we were friends with liked us, **and** respected our space.

They were never inappropriate or forceful—they just enjoyed our company. They were hands-off. After my sister and I stopped hanging out, I was nearly always by myself and usually at home. I was never afraid of any of the guys from our town though. I had an idealistic view of what life was about. I never imagined that anyone would try to hurt me.

One guy I liked later confided to me that when we first arrived from New Orleans, some of the fellows in town made him a bet that he wouldn't force me to be intimate with him . I remember that he had driven out to the local cemetery with me once. He confessed that he wouldn't do that to me. This was the young man who would later ask me to marry him and would possibly have been my husband had fate not intervened.

My life changed shortly after I graduated high school. I was 18 years old. My sister had bought one of her friends by my mom's trailer. I had never seen him before. He was short, dark-skinned and pretty good looking. I was at the sink washing dishes. My sister was dating her "babies daddy" at the time, so I didn't think she was seeing him. My sister left and went over to my grandma's house. She left us there to talk. He was ten years older than I was and fresh out of the army. He asked me out, so I said, "Yes!" He had a car too. We began to date, nothing serious to me, because I was really still in love with someone else that I had known for a longer time period. It was just something for me to do. I hung out for about two months with the new guy. He was nice to me. He would spend his money on me. We went to restaurants, to the mall and he bought me records and minor things I said that I wanted. He never made any moves on me at that time, but he did kiss me on the lips. I was comfortable and had no reason to be scared. I also never

thought that he wanted anything in return. I just thought he was being nice to me like the other guys we hung out with. I wasn't in love with him.

One night we went out in his car. He parked off the road off to the side near a cotton field. I remember it being summer. The moon was full. I can't remember everything very well, but he started removing my clothing, against my will. I begged him to stop. He forced me out of the car. It was dark and mosquitoes were out. We continued to wrestle back and forth, with me trying to keep my clothes and dignity and him trying to force me out of them. He won out, because he was stronger than I was—and we wrestled hard. He took advantage of me in the field that night, and my life was never the same. I didn't tell my mom or my sister what had happened to me. They had their own personal problems at that time and more than anything---I felt ashamed.

After that night, I felt sullied, dirty and fearful. I wasn't as happy as I used to be. I wouldn't walk through town like I used to. I was afraid that he was going to brag about it To everybody, and I would become a laughing stock. I felt unworthy and like I had lost the precious gift I was supposed to give my future husband. I thought that if someone looked at me, they could see it written all over my face, that I had changed. If I had told the local police it would be all over town and I'd be in the spotlight. It was the kind of attention I didn't need or ever want. I decided that he was going to have to marry me. I told him he would and we agreed to do that. It was an .Abraham situation.. Me trying to fix something and making it worse. I ended up with an Ishmael. Things went from bad to worse after that. He had been married before (but I didn't know how many times at the time). I really wasn't concerned either.

I found out that I knew very little about this man when we were dating. There was a monster in the closet. It was the beginning of an odyssey of abuse. I've heard it said that the dating process is designed to conceal information not reveal it. Anyone can be pleasant for a few hours, under the right circumstances. He took a job in another town to support us. His thumb got cut off when he was working on a machine. In ancient times, when someone stole something, they got a hand chopped off. He lost a finger. I figured it was a sign from God that he was being punished for stealing something that didn't belong to him.

A week before (*this happened*) the young man (*who took me to the cemetery*) and whom I really loved had asked me to marry him. I had no time to consider or accept the proposal. Before I could make a decision, the decision was made for me. My point is this, I'd lost something valuable to me, that I could never get back. I was gullible and in a situation with someone I shouldn't have been in. I had no idea what he was thinking about me or of what men could be capable of. I had a false sense of my own security and what the world is like, because no one ever talked to me about life and relationships with the opposite gender. I also made matters worse because I didn't wait on GOD to lead me and by trying to clean up the mess myself.

This was not the man I had waited for all of my life, he was my worst nightmare. I knew and now I know within myself that I deserved better and I REALLY was waiting for my prince. This man was not godly. As a matter of fact, I had no business out alone in a car with him or any other man at my age. I should not have accepted anything from him, because there aren't any "free lunches. in life. Everyone is not kind, gentle and well meaning, but I thought they were.

I understood how Dinah and Tamar must have felt. However, at least he was willing to be a Shechem and right the wrong committed. Know who you're dealing with, because one mistake in judgment can alter the course of your life. I got married and a lot of the guys who liked me didn't understand why. I sort of disappeared from view. Rape is never the woman's fault, but you never know how close you walk to danger each day. Many young women are raped by familiar people (family members or friends) not strangers. This is a wound that never heals because they don't seek counseling and because of the stigma and shame associated with rape. It's like having a large object fall on you. You don't want it to happen, but it does. Think about the situations you put yourself in. But remember that if something goes wrong, and you have made your wishes clear and said "No!" Then that male is to blame for the crime he perpetrates towards you. Also, don't fail to report your situation to the police or authorities.

CHAPTER 3 - The Strategizers v/s Sympathizers

In order to win a skirmish in war, one must know the enemy and his strategies. Believe me, the successful hunter knows his prey. Men observe and study women. They exchange information with their buddies. They recognize the signals and visual cues women give off. It's like intuition. Everyone has it. GOD gave us insight so that we could protect ourselves from danger.   Men use it so that they know when it's safe to approach a woman. They also use it to gain the upper hand in a relationship. Men listen to the grapevine to find out what other guys think of that female. In the battle that's waging between men and women, men are definitely winning!

I talked to an acquaintance who told me at one point in his life, he was dating more than 10 women at a time. This meant that someone was standing in line waiting to be abused. I believe him too. He said that something bad had happened to make him change his ways. It was the "*murder*". You know who I'm talking about. No one had to tell me that the girl he had killed was in love and obsessed with him and he was no doubt playing mind games with her to the point where she cracked. He said that she had the gun and was trying to shoot him and it went off accidentally and killed her. It almost signaled the end of his life, but he turned things around for himself.

As of this writing he lives with one woman but his phone rings constantly. The woman living with him has been conditioned not to ask a lot of questions. He makes it clear he doesn't want a jealous woman, because his job requires that he take a lot of calls (*Yeah! Right!*). He told her he was "in a meeting". That's what he calls it. Once while conversing with him, a female must have called him. His response to her was that he was in a meeting. He says that he's up front about having someone else (*if he does*) and that he doesn't hide it--

-there's no expectations as he put it. I told him, "*You're like a pack of cigarettes---smoke at your own risk.*" He's good at what he does because at the time that I talked to him, he was attentive, generous, and hospitable. He has the ability to make a woman feel as if she's the only person in the room. He told me that he often has to tell women "No thanks!" because women throw themselves at him. At one time he said that a girl broke into his cell phone to see who he'd been calling. Honestly, I think he enjoys the drama that he createsin his life, even though he says he doesn't. It's got to be flattering to have someone so obsessed with you that they're willing to go to all kinds of extremes. But that too can be a double-edged sword.

A male acquaintance once told me that's it's not normal for a man to be a monogamist. He said that monogamy is a learned behavior.
If this is true, then what are we to expect from relationships if a man has no higher power or God to direct his conscience? A Player has no real understanding that what he is doing is harmful to himself and to innocent women. The bible says that when a person "*fornicates*", one sins against their own body. I did not understand what that meant for a long time. Then it was revealed to me that when you partake of that kind of sin, you pollute your own temple (*the vessel in which you reside-your body*). It's not a sin outside of yourself, but something you have to live with (*within your spirit*). A Player isn't concerned with anyone's feelings or spiritual health. He just sees his behavior as a way to satisfy his need for power through mental manipulation. It's a serious game of mental chess.

One scheme males use like the one mentioned above, is what I call, "*the ploy of honesty*". A male pretends to be honest, with his dishonesty. So many women fall for this one. It's the bait married men (adulterers) and "*shackers*" use. A guy may be living with a female. He may be married or long-term "shacking up". He'll talk and fool around on the side with other women. He'll tell his side women that he isn't satisfied or happy at home. He doesn't commit to *the other woman* in his life, yet continues to play around with an affair. He uses their insecurities to manipulate them and have the best of both worlds. He says he's going to leave. He continues to complain about his home life. His strategy is to put up a false front of being *up-front* or *honest*. But what he's really asking is for you to put up with his situation until whenever! There's excitement and variety in the game for him. These men tell you they have someone at home, but the thing is, "I'm not happy!" This is a ploy to lure you into thinking that you have a future with him. Maybe he'll leave her one day, but that rarely happens, even with *the shackers*. Once a man has bonded with a woman, it's a hard tie to break! They don't like change and will stick with it, even if it's bad until most likely she decides to move on.

Another tactic men use is the *poor me*. *All I need is a good woman to save me* role. They use a woman's nature and what is really a strength against them.

By nature most women are ANTS:

a.) caretakers or nurturers

b.) hope-filled (hopeful) and forward thinkers.

c.) mentally tenacious or strong

d.) sensitive to the needs of others

Men have a tendency to be GRASSHOPPERS:

a.) mentally weak, egotistical and self- centered like young children

b.) NOW! oriented

c.) centered simplistic thinkers; comfort oriented

d.) adventurous, risk-takers

When a male senses that a woman is sympathetic, he tells her things that play on that sympathy. For example, he might be an alcoholic or a drug addict. There's something inside of her that thinks, *"Maybe he just hasn't met the right woman yet . If he loves me enough –he'll change for me."* There are men who major in manipulation. This man will come across as needy and pitiful and we fall for it. What woman needs a guy who's weaker than she is? We need real men, not more babies. Be careful of someone using your kindness and sympathy against you. Once you give your heart, you're in trouble!

or

Another deception I'll discuss is *"The Dream Guy* or the *Prince Charming* routine". He meets you and comes across as everything you ever wanted. He's going to feel you out to see what it is you want. You'll be observed and then assessed. He'll figure out what it is you're seeking in your relationships. For those first months or less (*until you become intimate*) he'll portray just that. When he knows that you're in love with him, then he'll show his true face. The remedy for this is to **WAIT** him out. Wait long enough and he'll show his true colors. The thing is that we often don't wait long enough. Time is the enemy of ignorance or rather lack of knowledge. Wait! Please wait and see what you're getting. Because once you've committed to someone, it's emotionally painful to extract yourself from the situation. I remember that once, I thought this guy was in love with me. I found out that he had ulterior motives, which came to light later on. It took great losses for me to come to my senses. It can cost a lot emotionally and financially.

Finally, I have to address the man who falls too quickly or who says, *"Let's get married!"* after a few dates. This is a sure sign that something's wrong. What's the big rush ? No one falls into love that quickly. Generally when a guy is in a hurry to get you bound up or committed he has security problems. Yeah, lust at first sight happens, but true love waits and as the bible says .love is patient.. He will respect your boundaries and take time to get to know you and allow you the same courtesy. Often these guys are jealous and insecure about themselves as men. They are controlling or wanting to gain control and feel that the best way to do that is to marry you. I've often had to tell guys to slow down. When they don't respect my boundaries, I'm ready to bail on them anyway. I don't like being forced to do anything. Do you?

ASSESSMENT CHAPTER 3

Why is a female's virtue so important?_____
_____
_____
_____

Dinah was the daughter of whom?_____

How did she lose her virtue?_____
_____

Explain how he tricked her family into accepting a marriage proposal:_____
_____
_____
_____

Whose sister was Tamar?_____

What happened to Tamar that ruined her
life?_____

_____
_____

Name two things that happens to a woman who is
violated?_____

_____

_____
_____

What does this saying mean? *"There is no free
lunch"?*_____

_____
_____

What should a woman avoid or be careful of when dating
males?_____

_____

What other decision could I have made to preserve (save) my
dignity or virtue?

_____
_____
_____

_____

In order to win a fight, what do you need to
know?_____

_____

How do men know if it's okay to approach a
woman?_____

_____

_____

Another word or synonym for a strategizer is: _____

Name one .ploy. men use to play
women:_____

_____

What makes a man a skilled
player:_____

What does "The Player" use to manipulate the women in his
life?_____

_____

_____

Which of these game strategies have been used against
you?_____

How did you deal with
it?_____

_____

_____

_____

Do you consider yourself wise or experienced when it comes
to males?_____ why do you say
this:_____

_____

CHAPTER 4 - The Game Cycle

I think any female of age has experienced the "*game cycle*". This is when a male does everything he can to impress you and get your attention. After he has won you –he no longer does those things. There is a cycle involved in conquest. When I was dating my ex-husband, he was generous when he had money. He was fresh out of the army with a pocketful of money. I told you he would buy me whatever I wanted. As times progressed ---- hard financial times came, he became less amiable and increasingly frustrated.

After the rape occurred and he felt fenced in by my request for marriage, he may have felt trapped. He became more jealous when we went to different places. He would accuse me of looking at other men. He became more brutal as well. After we were married, we didn't have a place to live. We couldn't live with his parents, because they lived in an overcrowded hovel. It was also unclean and really unfit. He hadn't settled into a stable job. We had to live in my mother's trailer for a short time. One night, for reasons I can't remember, he had gotten upset. We were in the backroom. My mom must have heard us arguing. He had an iron in his hand and was going to hit me in the face with it. My mother heard the commotion I guess and came into the room. She told him, *"No! you can't do that in here!"* What she meant was that there would be an even bigger fight if he did.

   During the game cycle there are three distinct phases that the relationship will go through. I'll label them stages A, B and C. Any relationship will go through these, even if they're true, because as time passes and people get to know one another they tend to relax. Genuine relationships don't go through the last phase.

A. WOOING- This is the first phase a man goes into after he sees a woman he's interested in. He attempts to establish a friendship or communication flow. He shows you that false face (*pretends to have the qualities you're looking for*). He's sizing you up for potential and to see what it is you want. He reads your signals. The dishonest guys all have a goal in mind (*a hidden agenda*). The end goal is to get with you for something. The thing this male is seeking may be companionship/partnership, money, sex, a place to live or perhaps all of the above. This is when he calls you everyday, maybe several times a day. He opens doors, pulls out chairs, pretends or is actually interested in what you like or don't like and makes an attempt to listen. The goal is to gain your attention, trust and confidence. This is half the battle!

B. CONQUEST - Is the second phase in the relationship mill. During this phase of the courtship, she has gained your trust, affection and a measure of your confidence although you are still getting to know one another. He moves in to take what he feels he has "*earned*" for his investment in you. This is where he feel comfortable asking for what he wants and is pretty sure he'll get it and he usually does if you're not on your P's & Q's. This is where many a female gives her all. This is where the hidden agenda starts to emerge or show itself. You have a level of intimacy. He doesn't call quite as much and you can catch the door yourself. He's comfortable with you and you with him.

C. RETREAT - In this final phase of the relationship, he has gotten as much as he wants from you. He doesn't call that much any more. He may begin to distance himself from you if he doesn't want a serious relationship. He visits less and separates himself from you to the point where you know it's over. You stand there wondering what happened to your prince. The man that you knew was your soul mate, your friend with whom you have so much in common is no longer there.

Take your time and find out who the real person is. Is he A or C? Find out why this person is interested in you. Do they want a long-term relationship or temporary use of you and your resources? Only time can reveal this to you.

Chapter 4 - The Ten Commands of Wise Women

In order to be a wise woman, who looks out for herself,
I think there are ten basic guidelines that you should follow
to help steer you in dealing with males:

(1). REMOTE locations are a NO-NO! If you're just
meeting a male, do so in a public place for a certain amount of
time. Try to keep from going to his apartment or car alone with
him, because you can easily get into a compromising
position. I dated a guy while I was in the service. He had
a friend named Derek. I wanted to plan a birthday party for
my boyfriend at the time. These guys had been tight for
some years. I told Derek that I wanted to plan a surprise
party for him.   He told me I could come over to his
apartment and plan. When I got over there, he was all
over me like a wet suit on a diver. I high tailed it out of
there as fast as I could. I told my boyfriend about it and he
(acted as if he) didn't believe me. I was hurt and
disappointed. I went with the best of intentions and things
could easily have spiraled out of control.

**(2). LISTEN to your first mind and the warnings or
misgivings you might have about any situation**. If it
doesn't feel right or safe--change your plans! Listen to
your heart and pay attention to the signals or things that
you see that aren't right about a guy. Don't dismiss them!

GOD gave you intuition and eyes so that you could be aware of what's happening around you for your own safety. I have seen things that told me about the person that I dismissed. I was dating my ex-husband, we would go to the city before we got married and he would stop at this building and he would go in and come on out. He was buying drugs at that time.

(3). SLOW DOWN - If he's in a rush to become physical, this is a danger or warning sign that he's not serious about you or a relationship. My question is always *"What's the hurry?" "Where are you going?"* This shows that this person is only concerned with his needs or wants and not what's good for you. Don't get so many stars in your eyes that you can't remember what's good for you down the road. Make sure your prince isn't a toad! If he can't respect your personal space or wishes this is a warning of what's to come. I hate it when a guy tries to touch all over me before I even know him. It's a turn-off and it makes me jumpy and uncomfortable around him. Males like that I dump fast. I like to take my time about things. Why should you be compelled to kiss a guy in the mouth on the first date? You shouldn't!

(4). MAINTAIN ORDER - Keep your life in order. When you get things out of order, you play catch up for the rest of your life. By this I mean that you should make sure that you can take care of yourself before anything or anybody else. Sometimes females get behind the 8-BALL because we don't have a good start in life and we perpetuate negative behaviors our parents may have started. Try not to have kids BEFORE you've finished school. Get married BEFORE you have children that you have to raise as a single parent. Get your high school diploma and learn a

good skill or trade . Don't start dating too early. It's a
distraction. It gets the mind all fuzzy and full of dreams
that might not really be!

(5). PAY YOUR OWN WAY- It's okay to pay your own way
sometimes, especially in the beginning of a relationship. Don't
expect too many freebies. If he asks you out on a date, then he
should be gentlemanly enough to pay for it, but a guy once told
me that a man respects a woman who pays sometimes. But,
never give the impression that you don't need his help.
It's a fine line to walk. Paying your way on occasion,
especially when you first meet, shows that you're
independent and not a gold-digger. If he wines and dines
you all the time--he may expect a pay off down the road. I
NEVER go anywhere without my own money. It makes
me feel confident and proud that I can fend for myself. A
former friend used to go out and she'd drag me along
even when we were broke. I hated it! She'd tell me how
she'd get them to buy her food or drinks. She was proud
of that and I was embarrassed. I didn't like her morals and
I found out she wasn't a respectable person on the inside
either. She used men like rags. When we'd go places
together, we never paid for anything. She'd charm the
money right out the fellows. I didn't like her philosophy of
life. I had my integrity and pride.

(6). OPPOSITES - Yes, they do attract one another, but what's
not said is that in the long run, differences in the important
things will lead to a lot of FRICTION on down the road. When
people first meet and the sparks are flying, they can't see
much else, but when a male is determining if a relationship
will be worth the long haul and commitment I think his
criteria is very different from a females. Both people really
need to have the same VALUE system. You both need to

believe that having goals and saving is important. Ask yourself, "*What evidence is there of this in his life*?" Is this person independent or dependent? Does he have morals or a belief in God? If not what will hold him in check or keep him from doing whatever he feels like. In my last serious relationship, he used to say that we had the same values, but what I saw in him wasn't what I believed. He drank, partied, gambled and hung out until all hours of the night . He lost a lot of his money gambling. I was trying to save money so that eventually I could buy my own home. He couldn't understand why I kept pulling away from him---I thought it was clear.

(7). DRESS APPROPRIATELY and respectfully. I'm not saying you have to wear a berka and headgear, but males may misconstrue how we dress. Guys draw conclusions about the way you dress. One "*young man*" I met when I was on my daily errands once told me that, "*A woman should let her inner beauty and personality show*". I was dressed just fine. Overall, his point was that provocative dress gave the wrong impression. Males are easily stimulated. I once heard a comedian remark in jest, " *If I'm wearing a policeman's uniform, people will think I'm a cop. So ladies don't dress like a tramp if you're not one*." What impression do you want males to have of you?

(8). OBSERVE FAMILY RELATIONSHIPS and background. If this person can't stay or live with their own family or is considered an outsider--BE CAREFUL! Find out why. Does the family trust him? If not why? Is this person still living at home (*not temporarily*) and not helping out with bills or planning for an independent future? If your own flesh and blood can't tolerate you, there's a problem. For example, there was this guy who couldn't live with his parents because he wouldn't work and was using drugs. They couldn't trust him in the house or trust him to be responsible. When he was on the prowl, he was looking for a female to take care of him. What do you think he was going to do to her? Use, abuse and disrupt her life.

(9). PRAY early in your life for God to direct your path regarding relationships as well as every thing else (*i.e. careers, friends, finances etc.*). There are forces out there making decisions about your future. You'd like the LORD to lead these. Ask the Lord to send a wholesome holy man who will love and respect you. A person who will help you be the best that you can be. Ask for wisdom in your choices. Every choice we make is like a fork in the road of life.

 (10). Pay ATTENTION to all warning signs and hints of this person's character. Don't dismiss things that might warn you as to what kind of person they are. What kinds of hints do they give off? Is this person insecure, selfish, responsible and reliable? What does his behavior say? Now is the time to flee if he really exhibits none of these traits.

Humanity Requires Certain Things

What do we need to be happy? In (1954) psychologist, Abraham Maslow developed a hierarchy of human needs. It starts from the bottom and works upward. If you look at how the pyramid is designed you see that, the most basic human needs start at the bottom:

(a.) PHYSIOLOGICAL NEEDS for food, shelter and nurturing from a parent.
(b.) SAFETY NEEDS cover relief from danger; a feeling of security.
(c.) BELONGING & LOVE NEEDS follow. We need to feel part of a family and social group. Perhaps this is why we have developed a society of axe murderers and sociopaths. Somewhere this need was lacking and they lash out to be heard. After all some attention is better than no attention according to some people (not me).
(d.) ESTEEM NEEDS mean that individuals require a measure of respect for who they are and what they've accomplished.

The other four needs above Physiological, Safety, Belonging and Esteem :
The Need to Know/Understand; Aesthetic Needs (Beauty and Order); Self Actualization and at the very Top of the pyramid is Transcendence. These needs are almost secondary to the four listed above. Wouldn't you agree?
Security, companionship, belonging and respect are needs that are satisfied through good, wholesome, complimentary relationships with other people. There's a different dynamic associated with male/female relationships as opposed to female/female friendships. This is because we're two halves of what make a whole in God's plan. There are

people who gave up on life because they never felt a sense of belonging and love---not in their families or personal love lives. Who wants to be lonely? It's like being an outcast. However, it's very important that we not compromise our future for "*fools gold*". God has even said, "It's not good that man should be alone." In a 1950's Bette Davis film entitled, "*Ms. Skeffington*", the wife was a beautiful, social butterfly, who had many suitors when she was young and pretty. Out of necessity, she married an older man named Mr. Skeffington who loved her dearly. He would always say to her, " *A woman is most beautiful when she's loved*." He attended to her every need and desire. She would berate and ignore him. Toward the end of the movie after she'd gotten older and less desirable, she realized what he'd meant to her and how important he'd been to her. One could also understand the quote above. We can't deny that there's a light that radiates from the heart and spirit when we feel desirable and loved. There's no substitute for the real thing!!! True love will wait and it endures hard times. Wait for him and make him wait for you.

Chapter 4 - Assessment

1. What's the first phase in the game cycle?_____

_____

2. What does it mean when he shows a "false face"?_____

_____

3. Name two things that can be on the hidden agenda:_____

_____

_____

4. In the second phase of the game cycle you have a level of what?_____ What is *clear* or apparent here?_____

_____

5. In which phase of the game cycle has the male gained your trust?_____

In which phase of the cycle is his hidden agenda still a secret to you?_____

6. SELAH :Have you ever experienced these cycles?_____ If so, which ones and how did you feel at each level (*You don't have to write that here, but think about it in your heart or you can share it with your study*

mates)

_____

_____

_____

_____

_____

7. What's a danger signal stated in the "Ten Commands of a Wise Women?"_____

_____

_____

_____

_____

8. In your own words, state or sum up the 7th Command of a Wise Woman:_____

_____

_____

_____

9. When did Abraham Maslow develop the "*Hierarchy of Needs*"?_____ (year) What's at the very bottom of the pyramid?_____ Which need(s) relate to relationships?_____

10. Name one need that must be met on Level #1:_____

11. Do you think you're attracting the wrong kind of males?_____ If so why? (*refer to the 10 Commands of*

a Wise Woman to answer this question) Are you breaking any or all of these guidelines for building a healthy relationship ?_____

_____

_____

_____

12. Do you think you're viewed as a respectable female or easy?_____Explain why for either answer:_____

_____

_____

_____

Make A List & Check It Twice!

The best way to get what you're looking for in the store or not to forget what you came there for-- is to make a grocery list before you go. Often, it's not until we get much older and have had experiences (*good and bad*), that we realize what it is we've wanted in a mate. It's also as we grow older as women that we gain experience and become more confident and practical about life and living. When I was younger, I wasn't often approached by guys. I would think that the last fellow who showed interest in me would actually be the last one. I was pretty, but I didn't get asked to dance a lot. I told you that before I reached the age of sixteen, I was just a pair of eyes and legs. Not particularly attractive.

After age sixteen, I blossomed into a fair young lady. Many females will go through this awkward stage. This is when self image is forming and we might get teased a lot or not look particularly attractive. However, "*This too shall pass.*" I've found that we all pass through physical and emotional stages in life. More often than not, "*The ugly duckling does turn into a swan!*" So don't be too hard on yourself because you might not feel that you compare to others. We're unique in our own right.

I want to share this story about a boy named Elmo:
"Elmo worked in Mr. Kramer's grocery store down the street from where I lived in New Orleans. I went to that store every other day and got things I wanted or that our family needed. Elmo never talked to anyone. He wore black, dorky glasses and had an afro. He had bucked teeth. He was quite unattractive and unsociable. He was in the background all the time. Never speaking or talking except out of necessity. He'd do his job and never exchanged as much as a glance. After my parents divorced, the family left New Orleans in the late 70's. I went to high school and graduated. I decided to travel back to LA to find my dad so that I could start college . I went to the old neighborhood and looked around. Many of the friends we had known had moved on. The most popular family was "The Robinson's". To us they were like the Jackson's. Some were still there and some had grown up, went to college and/or started families. I went down to Mr. Kramer's store to see how much it had changed and do you know Elmo was still working there--while attending college? He had matured and grown up. I can't leave out the fact that he had morphed into a fine, physical specimen!

I would not have known it was Elmo if Mr. Kramer not called his name. He was absolutely gorgeous!" The afro and bucked-teeth were gone. I couldn't believe it nor will I ever forget it. He had changed so much physically, but his personality was still the same. He was hard working, faithful, self-directed, disciplined and sure to make some girl a great husband. I walked away with my jaw on the ground and as you can see, to this day I'm still dumbfounded.

I talk about this because none of us will ever really know what we can or may become in the future. Think of yourself as "*a work in progress*". You can always get better. Confidence in oneself is developed over time. I have knowledge of who I am. Nobody can take that away from you or I if we really believe in ourselves. I've learned what I have to offer another person as well as the world. I've also learned to be content even if I'm alone. I have dry spells, but it's okay. I have more peace during those times. Dealing with someone who's not only different from you physically as well as mentally takes a lot of energy. That's why marriage is so much work, combined with the fact that human beings tend to be selfish if that characteristic is not tempered by a firm spiritual foundation.

In school, I was talking to the students about adjectives---I was telling them that an adjective not only covers color, size, number, and shape, but behaviors and feelings too. Some students tried applying these internal human characteristics to inanimate objects. I asked them, can a stone be angry or smart? There's a difference between describing an inanimate object and a human being. Humans possess more than outward appearances. GOD has given us gifts and qualities that make us special. Try not to take a life time discovering what GOD has given you. Don't be so insecure that you feel you have to compromise to impress anyone else. Be true to yourself.

A WISH LIST

A grocery list for the perfect person requires that you sit down and decide what your list would look like. Physical qualities are less important in the long haul.

What are they? Here's a look at my list:

1). Has faith in God
2). Someone I can be myself with. I don't have to be afraid that they will take advantage of my caring, nurturing nature. I don't have to be tough with them to get them to do the things they need to.
3). Doesn't use drugs as a crutch (*alcohol, opiates*)
4). Loves me unconditionally--whether I'm fat or thin; sick or well.
5). Is encouraging and helping me to follow my dreams.
6). Attractive to me and I to him.
7). Patient
8). Sensitive to how I feel; a good listener.
9). The person is honest and not prone to exaggeration or lying.
10). Hard working
11). Proud in a good way (*too proud to let a woman be the sole bread-winner*) or let someone else take care of his responsibilities. Not boastful or so insecure that he has to show off at every turn.
12). Caring toward others who're not just his family.
13). Has a job and good transportation.

14). Makes me feel secure and will look out for my best interests.

Chapter 5 - What Do Men Like?

You can name some of the most beautiful and successful women in the world. Marilyn, Halle, Brittany, Janet, you, me and scores. What do we have in common? You guessed it ---- hard times when it came to the men in their lives. We can be counted as some of the most beautiful, intelligent, successful women in the world, yet no one is exempt from the experience of a failed relationship and heartbreak. You can say that Marilyn literally gave up on life because of this.

These women had money, looks and success it wasn't enough for the men in their lives. Beauty or success isn't a guarantee that a woman will find love and happiness. Marilyn Monroe was one of the most beautiful women and still considered a sex symbol after her death so many years later. Yet, she was lonely and unhappy. In the bible, women like Sara (Abraham's wife), fell into a snare because of their looks. When Abraham went down into Egypt, he told a lie and said that Sarah wasn't his wife because she was so attractive and he feared that because she was so, the Egyptian royal would try to take her. Bathsheba was desired by King David because he looked upon her and wanted her, so sometimes a woman's looks can become a snare or trap. The man may not be sure he wants her for arm candy or for internal reasons. Looks don't guarantee a successful relationship or union. On the other hand, Rachel and Queen Esther were favored because of their looks in a positive way. When Jacob went to work for Laban, the father of Rachel, he worked twice the time he should have to gain her hand. The scripture says of Rachel in Genesis Chapter 29:17, 20 ...."Leah was tender eyed; but Rachel was beautiful and well favored.. and Jacob served seven years for Rachel;

and they seemed unto him but a few days, for the love he had to her."

Queen Esther was able to deliver the Israelite people because she caught the eye of the prince who held her people in captivity. She gained favor because she was godly and virtuous and God used her to deliver them (*the Jews*) from death. Esther Chapter 2:7-9, ..."*for she had neither father nor mother, and the maid was fair and beautiful.*" You see, God had a plan for each of these women's lives. They were not only beautiful outwardly, but also inwardly. They had a heart toward the things of God and he used them in a powerful way. I have a saying, "*I'd rather be ugly on the outside than ugly on the inside.*" It's not so easy to rid oneself of an ugly heart and soul.

This chapter is about what men want. Honestly, I don't know what that is. If I could fully and truthfully answer that question, I'd be the most sought after woman in America. But, when one has questions, the best way of answering those questions is by using the scientific method of inquiry. Observe and then draw an inference or conclusion. Your situational observation skills will make or break you. I'll share some of the insights and conclusions I've come to. No matter what nationality or group--- an attractive woman still can turn men's heads. However looks alone isn't enough to hold a man's attention or guarantee a long, fruitful relationship. Rich men like trophy wives *(beautiful women)*, women of status *(societal position)*, or the women they've been with before they became rich and famous. Women represent status of one sort or another.

A woman with a shapely figure *(small waist and full hips)* is desirable at first glance. But, I've met men who like a certain body type *(not necessarily of that sort)*. These are superficial things to say the least, perhaps that's why Americans are so busy relationship jumping. There's a "*code of silence*" among men, so they aren't very forthcoming with information about their secrets. They'll share information about the latest ploys amongst themselves, but not too readily with women. Men are simple/sensitive creatures. Therefore they like simple things. When dealing with a man, the biggest thing in the room will be his ego. He doesn't want anything or anyone to outshine or outdo him. He needs lots of praise and positive affirmation or he God made him that way and that's the way he'll stay.

Men are attracted to a certain personality type. I've observed that African-American men seem to prefer women who are authoritarian or who take a direct leadership role in the relationship, A female who tells them exactly what it is they want or expect (no guessing involved). The key is knowing how to go about doing this, without injuring the pride.

The next observation is that the average guy prefers females who are not highly talkative. Even well educated men tend to be this way. Men with less education or social status may be intimidated or are made uncomfortable by braininess or talkativeness in women. Talkativeness tends to be viewed as a distraction. Most fellows want a little peace when they come in from the world at large.

But they will communicate with a loved one, again, this is not for the exceptional fellows, but the heels.

Men also don't like to be controlled or feel boxed in by a woman who's overly insecure. They rebel by seeking attention from women outside of the relationship if a woman is too controlling, possessive or jealous. Men don't want an emotionally needy woman. I could say that Marilyn was a needy woman. She was constantly concerned about aging because she felt that her appeal was tied to her physical beauty. She wanted security and closeness, but the very thing that made her desirable became a trap. She was viewed as eye-candy and not as a whole person. Men tend to shy away from women who are insecure and need constant reassurance. It's best to know who you are before you try to have a relationship with somebody else.

The wise man likes a woman who can take care of herself, but he also likes a woman to need him as well. A smart woman knows how to balance her ego against his. Some men are threatened by women with a lot of education unless they are comparably educated, but you don't have to be college educated to gain respect. You just need to be wise and respect yourself. Don't let some guy use and abuse you—they won't like you for it! They also can smell if you're after them for their money. Only emotionally insecure men try to buy a woman's affection.

A male doesn't want to plan a future with someone he can't trust. You need to be a trustworthy, pillar of virtue in his eyes. If a man loses respect for you, it's hardly ever regained, because many men have a double standard when it comes to cheating or infidelity. They think it's okay for a man to cheat, but not a woman. Let me share this example with you:

"This story is about Paul. He and his wife met and married while they were in the military. Toward the end of her duty tour they got separated. Orders came through that she had put in before they'd met. She was planning to go to Korea to be with a guy she had met before they'd gotten together. She never told him that though. When she met her husband she felt that she was in love and no longer wanted to be with the other guy. She got sent overseas anyway and her new spouse was left here in the states. They called and wrote one another all the time. But the pain of the separation was immense for them both.

They were newlyweds—and it was very important for their relationship to grow during those early stages. She said that she was heartbroken to have to leave him, because she loved him. He kept urging her to get out, but she had to stay on that tour of duty for at least six months before she could return to the states. The tour was for one full year. Finally, she was able to submit papers and get out on a hardship separation. Which meant that she couldn't go back into the service any more. They reunited after she returned to the states. He was an insecure man as it was, and he kept questioning her about what had happened over there. He wanted information as to what happened while she was gone. He confessed to her that he'd cheated on her while she was gone. He'd been with a girl that he'd known before he met her. She knew he was telling the truth because she told me that she had an STD that she hadn't had before. She said that she had wanted to talk to him about it, but that her conscience was bothering her too because she had cheated on him. Yes, she had cheated on him with the guy she'd known before him. She told me that overseas everybody from America had a different (lower) standard of morality than normal, *because most of those people missed home so much, that they would try to find comfort any way they could. The culture, the country, the foods, the sights and sounds were so foreign and strange—and it was difficult for someone to be there because it was like being a world away. One way of relieving that anxiety was to be with someone who might not be your betrothed. That's what she did. She told him what she did! It was a BIG mistake. He never let her live it down and it drove a permanent wedge between them for the rest of the marriage. Later on he recanted his statement and swore that he never cheated. Eventually, the marriage broke down because of his constant accusations and paranoia . She said that she forgave his infidelity, because she loved him, but he never forgave or FORGOT hers. The "affair" was always coming up when there was a problem. Instead of alleviating jealousy, it fed the flames. He began accusing her all the time of different things. Finally, it got so bad that they separated and eventually divorced. She said she couldn't take the questionings all the time about where she was and what she was doing"*

Guys don't like easy women. As I've said before, "*Why buy the cow when you can get the milk for free*?" You definitely won't be the one he takes home to momma if all the guys are talking about having been with you. However some fellows have a tendency to prefer those kinds of females but the drawback is that it's usually a financial arrangement. Men can cheat, but they expect their women to be the pillars of society and piety, and my advice is if you do mess up, it's best to tell the LORD and leave it at the altar. God will forgive you quicker than an injured male. Guilt can be a powerful manipulative. It gives the offended the upper hand in a relationship.
I'd like to thank all the young men who were kind enough to

share their thoughts about relationships between males and females.

Here's what the guys I questioned said about females:

> "When we exchange phone numbers, they (females) need to wait a few days before calling me. When they call too soon, it makes them seem too eager or desperate."

> "If you break up with a guy, make it clean, because if you try to stay friends with them. The new guy is going to think you're still being intimate with him."

> "It's harder for a man to be friends with a woman."

> "A woman can be friends with a guy, without being intimate with him. When they share a common interest."

> "Make a guy wait at least 4-5 months before having sex with him. The minimum is 3 months."

> "Make him wait! The longer you make a guy wait to be with you, the more respect he'll have for you, because he knows you made the other guys wait too. He will be more willing to marry you than the girl who gave it up to him the first night, because you made him wait. He'll have this opinion of you even if he's with someone else—while he's waiting for you."

> "Don't expect him to spend so much money in the beginning going out."

> "Guys will try to date you and your friends."

"A man likes to be satisfied---cook my dinner, run my bath water , stuff like that."

"Don't be afraid to go over to a guys house. Get to know his family, check him out. Watch his activity patterns, if it changes—then you know he's cheating."

"When you go on a first date with a guy, sometimes it's good to have a friend go along with you, because he could be a rapist or a stalker. Don't let a guy know where you live right away."

"Don't have unprotected sex if you're married or in a committed relationship."

"Men play around because of pride. It's about winning and being on top. Some guys make bets. I don't make bets because I have sisters."

"After some guys get with a girl, they despise them and look for a reason to break up, so they cheat."
"If you get into a relationship, he needs to have some type of income and religion."

"Women shouldn't get so caught up in emotion that they can't see reality. I knew this lady, and she was seeing a married guy. On holidays he would never be with her. He always had an excuse. You'll be with the one you really want or care about."

"One lie leads to another."

"If a guy knows all your friends, it's not a good sign."

"Guys will try to date you and your friends."

"Never sell your boyfriend to your friends, because they might be scoping him out for themselves."

"I have daughters. I tell her to make sure a guy has a job and a car, because if he doesn't have transportation, he'll be putting wear and tear on yours. Also make sure he's clean."

Chapter 5 – Assessment

1. Name at least one famous female that you've heard of or read about in the news who's had a lot of relationship problems:_____ Explain what you think the problem is

:_____

_____

_____

_____

What would you suggest that she could do?_____

_____

_____

_____

2. Name one biblical character (woman) who found favor because of her looks?_____

_____

_____

3. What is meant by the term "trophy" wife:_____

_____

_____

_____

4. In the beginning of a relationship, what gets a males attention?_____ Does this keep his

attention?_____ Why or why
not?_____
_____
_____

5. Why is it important for a female to be able to take care
of herself even if she's in a
relationship?_____

_____
_____

6. What is one of the most important traits a woman must
have to keep a relationship
going?_____

_____

7. Name three things men don't like in a female their
involved with:

a._____

b._____

c._____

8. If a female is bossy, over possessive, and insecure, what
can this cause a man to
do?_____

_____

9. A female SHOULD wait until she's married to become
intimate with a mate. However, because of the speed at
which relationships move in our culture that seldom
happens, but according to what guys say-- How long
should a female wait before becoming intimate with a
male?_____ months or years (circle one).

10. Complete the following quote from this chapter, " *The longer you make a guy _____ to be with you , the more _____ he'll have for you because he _____ you made the other guys _____ too.*"

Chapter 6 - Always the Wrong Guy? You Wonder Why?

Have you ever met a person who's never had a successful, long term relationship? I'm sure we all know someone who can't keep anybody. Remember in the dedication, I said that some of us will never have a lasting relationship because we've crapped out in the game. One sure fire way to end up with nothing is not to value what God gave you and be aware of the gifts that have been placed within you for stewardship. Treasure your body, your soul and the gifts that God placed inside of you.

It would be nice if there was a camp for wounded women. Not a cult, but a place where women could come to escape the constant demands, expectations, hurt, harm and abuse from those who are supposed to love them.

We need to take time to heal ourselves before we jump into other commitments. Find out what makes us tick and stop being afraid of spending some quality time with ourselves. Time away from society to seek a higher spiritual enlightenment is a worthwhile investment. We put too much emphasis on *"being in love."*

I've never seen anyone who values themselves as little as many women (and some of the men who're supposed to love them). It took me years to finally figure out that I had so much to offer friends and a future mate. I was scared, scarred and unhealthy inside. I wouldn't have known love if it had fallen on me. I didn't know what real love looked like, because I'd never experienced it. I also didn't know what I wanted or needed. If I was to put in one word, what I'd like it would be SECURITY. Security covers a lot of things! I'd like the security to be myself, to know that I'd be safe with this person. Also know that I have prepared for a comfortable future.

When we're constantly attracting the wrong types

people to us on a continual basis, perhaps it's happening for spiritual reasons that we don't understand or recognize. When I was younger, my cousin came to visit . We were discussing relationships and I explained some of my dilemma. She said to me, "*You're attracting guys who want a caretaker—you need to look into that.*" I've thought back on that comment quite often. Yes, I do tend to take care of people. Males often referred to me as "sweet or nice". I was never sure what it was about me that they see that makes them think I'm nice. Is it something I'm wearing? Of course not! It's that keen sense of observation I referred to earlier that enables them to scope me out. My mom and I have similar values when it comes to Christianity. I have relatives who've never set foot inside of a church although they say they believe in God. They never read their bible or behave in a godly way. I'm not saying that makes you a Christian, what I'm saying is that on a deeper level, there's something in their behavior that makes me know they don't really take God's word to heart, this becomes evident in their negative actions. Although a person's mouth says they believe in God their daily actions say otherwise.

There's an uneasiness in my spirit when I'm around them. I can't explain what it is, but something's just not right. I told mom that when people get along well, it's because their hearts and spirits agree. Generally they both have the same measure of caring heart, philosophy of life or other spiritual values. The bible asks, "*What fellowship hath light with darkness*?" It's true, when people have opposing spiritual views--- they clash and the reverse occurs (*when they're the same, they get along*).

In the relationship world, often "opposites attract." What do you think the results are or would be if a church girl started dating a drug addict? How about a good student who dates a drop-out? How would a neat person get along if they marry a hoarder? How about a free-spirit and a control freak? How about a bum and hard-worker? Yes, opposites do attract a person, but you should be able to infer that when people have too much of a varied personality, there will be problems and annoyances. The wrong people could be coming to us because of that reason.

Darkness is sometimes seeking light and vice-versa. On a deeper level, a male may be attracted to you because of the positive spiritual energy you radiate. For example, you might be: fun-loving, generous, caring, nurturing and have all sorts of other great character traits. Nine out of ten times, the guys you'll attract will be the opposite. On the surface they might come across as being like you, but as he reveals himself you find that he's different. I've never seen anyone who values themselves as little as some women and the men that they care about. This is particularly true in the African-American community. I think that the absence of father figures to show young males how to behave has hurt us a lot. The girls have no father figure to affirm and reassure them that they're wonderful and the males have no good examples to follow. It took me years to figure out what I had to offer anyone. I was emotionally unhealthy because as a child the only things I'd seen were negative images of relationships. My parents argued and fought all the time. My mom would catch my dad cheating on her and she'd chase him down with a butcher knife and try to kill him. I seldom remember them talking and relating in a healthy way.

Remember that I've said I was all arms, legs and eyes. I wasn't popular. As a matter of fact I was invisible. I had two friends and one was my T.V. set. It wasn't until I turned sixteen that I really had to deal with issues regarding males. I can remember on the eve of my maidenhood my dreamboat. His name was Perry. "I was scared of boys because of the incident in New Orleans involving "the kiss".

After my parents separated in New Orleans, my dad moved to Kenner. He'd met a woman he had started living with. Definitely the end of the marriage. I went to live with my dad. We went to church out there. The pastor had an adopted son named Perry. Perry was F-I-N-E! He was dating one of the girls in the choir named Sylvia. Sylvia was mature looking for her age and so was Perry. We kids were all in the choir. I had such a crush on him. I remember Perry because he was popular and played football. He was gorgeous in anyone's book. The church would take the choir on trips to sing. Perry was in the choir too. On occasion I would daydream about him, but never harbored any real hope that he'd be interested in me. One day I'd gone to the Pastor's house to take the First Lady something. Perry was outside skimming the pool with a net. As I stood there watching, he came over to me--said something. He stood very close. I got very nervous. He leaned in and kissed me on the lips. Then I got so nervous, that I sat down in a chair on the deck. It was full of water! The back of my shorts were soaking wet. I stood up, said good-bye and backed out of the gate. I ran home coursing with emotions, but the main one was fear. Shortly thereafter, I ended up leaving LA, but that day made me hopeful, at the same time scared. It reinforced the idea that maybe I was attractive to someone. But I also know that to Perry, I could have just been another "entree on the menu".   He was mature and most likely a hunter. The fear that I had

about being French kissed once again probably saved me.
I never went back down there because I was mortified and
at the same time hopeful that someone would be
interested in me. I never knew if I had a type or not.

When you're young, those things aren't evident. I was
too young and unskilled to know. Now, I know that a certain
type of male is attracted to me. Some of us have a hard
time with finding a suitable mate or partner because there
are so few eligible guys left out there. Women have had
to take on the roles that men traditionally occupied and
this has left men castrated and seeking ways to make
themselves feel strong.

When we do meet a guy, he may have the same
character traits or tendencies as the last guy we dated.
If we're attracting the same type of person over and
over again, perhaps it's because of some kind of
energy we're putting out there. No, this isn't New
Age ! People are drawn to us for one of two reasons
on a spiritual level. It's because we're giving off light or
darkness. When I say this, let's say that LIGHT comes
from the positivity that emanates from our spirit. For
example, you might be a confident, high spirited, amiable,
and generous person. Of course people will be attracted to
you for those reasons. Who wouldn't want to be around
someone like that.

On the other hand, if you're a female who has
insecurity issues which are evident by the way she
uses foul language, is short-tempered, impatient, and
dressed in a provocative way. There is a negative energy
or darkness evident in their life. We attract darkness
when we feel poorly about ourselves. Much like a
wounded fish in a sea of sharks, they smell the blood and
sense that. Don't you have that ability to sense things

about other people? Each person has this sense-ability for their protection. However, there is the flip-side to this. This discernment can be used to gage a person's vulnerability.

If a male is seeking a woman that he can take advantage of, he's going to be looking for one of the two types of women. He's going to be looking for a generous caring woman or a female that feels poorly about herself. The difference is that one gives off LIGHT and the other DARKNESS. The difference between the two is the motive that drives their actions. If a person is giving off positive energy (LIGHT), then she's doing what she does out of the abundance of love and goodness God put into her heart, but if she's doing what she does because she's insecure and wants to hold onto or capture a man's affection it's DARK. If a male is willing to use a female for what he can get from her, what kind of energy do you think he has? Two negatives can't make a positive in that situation. That only happens in algebra .

People always referred to me as a "*nice person*." Sometimes it used to offend me because I wanted to be thought of as tough. In Satan's world, "*It's survival of the fittest*". Meaning that you claw your way to the top by climbing over as many bodies as needful. In God's world "*The meek shall inherit the Earth." I prefer to go with God's plan. I've always handled matters with this philosophy of life , "Love thy neighbor as thyself*". I would like to think that I deal with others as I would want someone to deal with me if I were in their situation. My first instinct is to take care of some one else. I think my good side outweighs my bad side by quite a bit, but I feel like we all need to be able to *'give 'em hell* when the need arises.

I began to ponder what it is about me that makes

people think I'm nice. I assessed myself and the things that I can put my finger on are that I'm willing to help out and I have a teamwork mentality, when it comes to getting a job done. I believe in sharing out of my abundance or lack thereof, if someone has less than I do. I believe you should help someone develop their dreams and God will enable you to do the same if you're unselfish. Those are the key qualities that come to mind. So, being a do-gooder isn't so bad, but it's those same qualities that can draw people who are the exact opposite and they're looking for someone to victimize. As stated before, a female has to be careful and assess why someone is interested in her. Are you attracting someone with a darkness of spirit ?

When I was a young girl, I had a diary. I used to write in it on occasion. Shortly after I graduated from high school and moved to Ohio where I was attending college, I found my diary among my clothes. It was a few years old. I looked over it and as I read, I couldn't believe some of the junk I'd written. Boy, was I vain and full of myself (*youth*). I talked about how lucky one of my suitors would be to get me and about how attractive I was. I'd stand in front of the mirror and admire myself. How could any guy not like me? By the same token, I was really very insecure. The values and goals that I had set for myself, resulted in my spending lots of time alone. But it wasn't so hard for me as long as I knew I was on the right path. Having a virtuous nature and a clean heart make you feel strong and happy. When you feel used and dirty, it overshadows your confidence. Because you know that you've disappointed yourself and God. I used to be so happy !

As I've said before, people are attracted to us for one of two reasons. There is a light or a darkness that they're attracted to. I felt alone even when I was in relationships or married because I couldn't trust the person I was involved with to be faithful or protective. They didn't make wise decisions. They were chosen as my mates for the wrong reasons. I married my first husband out of necessity. He was a wife-beater and serial cheater. The second marriage was to a well-meaning, extremely insecure coke addict. He did do romantic things, but his insecurity wore thin. He would ask me how I felt about matters and when I told him, he'd interpret my feelings and it wasn't what I'd told him. I married him because I was lonely and had been alone for a while. He knew before I did that I really didn't love him. No one else seemed interested in me. I didn't respect the authority of either spouse, and I couldn't trust them to lead me around a corner. No one was in tune with how I felt, including me.

I was radiating darkness because my motives for choosing my mate was wrong. I felt like no one would ever really want me. I had extremely low self-esteem. I didn't feel attractive or worth much. Very few fellows ever approached me. Perhaps I was giving off this vibe that said , "STAY CLEAR! DON'T TOUCH! NERVOUS TYPE". Growing up no one ever seemed to like me enough to stick it out and hang around--even though I was different. I had a label that came with me. I realized much later in my life, that I preferred a specific kind of guy. They were blue collar, short, dark, men. These men, because of their height were very insecure, but had a strong penchant for my physical type. I'd always been approached by the same type of guy.

Secondly, I felt threatened by tall men. I had this idea that they could overpower me. Somehow they'd be stronger. That can't be far from the truth. Short men seemed less threatening. But quite the contrary, short men have an inferiority issue or complex. They feel that they have to prove themselves by being the louder, fiercer and more ostentatious than their counterparts. They don't want to appear weak to others.

Finally, I preferred men with blue-collar background because it was comfortable for me. I felt that professional guys would be judgmental of me because I'm not ambitious enough for them. Perhaps I didn't have enough drive to make it to the top of the ladder.

As you can see, most of my conceptions and choices were colored by negative ideas about myself and others. My motives were influenced by these negatives. They had some power over me to the extent that I let them. That's why it's important to know why you do the things you do. Know yourself and what motivates your decisions and choices in life. When something isn't working positively in your life, examine it and find out why.

This information is not meant for those great guys out there. This book is for the rules and not the exceptions to it. We must take as much control over our future as we can through wise counsel and prayer. I repeat "and prayer". There may be a room full of guys and the crazy one will want to hook up with you. If you know you're not crazy, what does he want with you? Perhaps what that person is looking for is some stabilizing or soothing agent in their lives. Some compassion and love that they've been missing. However we can't lose sight of what we need and start playing doctor. That person needs God in their life, and if they can't add something positive to your life, that person can't be right for you.

Relationships can start off simply and get out of hand quickly. One final point about the extent to which a females weaknesscan ruin not only her life, but those of her children is my final vignette.   A girl that I grew up with, was dating her first cousin's boyfriend. This started when we were all teenagers. He was a serial philanderer, not only was he dating them, but when we were in school together, he began an affair with a classmate of mine. He was a busy guy. The second choice of the two cousins, I will have to call "Miss X." What else can I call her? Always took second place to her fairer, light-skinned, more attractive cousin.

As they matured, he decided to get married, you can guess who he chose to be his wife. After the marriage, the rejected woman (*Miss X*) still continued to sleep with him. There was no shame even after this public rejection. Both cousins eventually had children by him, one set was legally, publicly and openly acknowledged, while the illegitimate children of Miss X. were ignored and disowned.

He provided no money or emotional support to help Miss X. raise *her* children. It is doubtful that she ever told the kids who their real father was because she did not want them confronting him or going around town telling people this secret. He bought a nice home for his wife to live in and gave her every good thing he could afford. His wife was able to stay home and raise her children. His wife shut her eyes to the affair. She knew it was going on. The two cousins even hung around together. The wife accepted his cheating with others as well. She was provided for but never asked questions in return for this life. Miss X. would "*shadow*" his wife and has continued to be his concubine for over thirty years. This situation has been a curse for Miss X. and her children. I can't imagine her ever being happy. Every day of her life she's been less than an honorable mention. The children suffered most from what I can tell. Miss X. gave him a son that his wife could not. A son he doesn't openly acknowledge.

Everyone in town knows about this absurdity. It's the most well-known secret around. Do you think he loves either one of these women? Explain why or why not. Do you think this situation is okay because men will cheat? How do you think Miss X. should feel after over thirty years of being someone's rug? This is another real-life example of how little women value themselves. I'm sure he gets lots of props or "*atta boy's*" from the guys for this behavior.

Chapter 7 – Tips & Loose Ends

(1). **Understand that God made men and women different mentally and physically**. My ex-husband is the same weight as when I met him, smaller. I've gained quite a few pounds over the years. This is a minor example of how we differ. The mental component is the most variable aspect of our personalities and most important to understand and consider when dating.

2). **Sex for the majority of males is about variety, pride, and possession**. They can cheat and feel that they haven't wronged the female who had confidence in them. *They separate their feelings from their physical actions*. Men also "*mark*" their territory by way of this act. They get possessive if they care for you. They can also be with you physically and not care if they ever see you again. A male won't become possessive or obsessive about a female until he's been intimate with her. It's also then, that he reveals his true nature. Who he actually is. It's the opposite for women. If a female (*a real woman*) is intimate with a guy, she thinks of that as a commitment.

(3). **If you CHEAT, I'm of the opinion that it's best not to tell him, if he's unbalanced**. If you're married, it may eat away at you—but you have to weigh the benefit against the cost. God will forgive you, but he may not. It will depend upon the type of man he is. His pride ego will have been injured and you won't ever be able to live it down. He'll spend the rest of his life trying to get even with you. When someone has knowledge regarding another person's guilt, it gives them the upper hand, especially in relationships. Some one can play on that. If he knows you were unfaithful, he can use it against you for a long time. There can also be this "*one upmanship*". If she cheated on me then I can cheat on her. Take your sins to GOD and leave them there! There's a double standard about cheating even though men like to think they are liberal minded.

(4). **He seldom shows his true self until he's slept with you.** If there's a demon in the closet, it comes out after your clothes have come off. **Wait him out!** Find out who you're dealing with, because once you've given your heart -- you're sunk. As I've said before if he's sincere--what's the hurry? He won't respect you for giving yourself away too easily anyway. LOVE and RESPECT yourself above any man. I see so many girls and women who don't do this--that's the reason I wrote this book. A guy told me that, "We don't tell the good girl's secrets." Remain one of the good girls.   Sex has a lot of emotional and spiritual consequences. There are chemicals within our bodies that promote the bonding experience. Also diseases and loose character take a toll on the body and heart.   It sounds old fashioned, but has the way we've been doing business turned out very well? No!

(5). **Stay celibate as long as you can**. It's never too late to rededicate your life and body to the Lord and clean living. Knowing you're clean and are saving yourself for someone special gives you a certain inner beauty and strength. When you give yourself to someone who's not worthy of you, you feel used and unhappy. If a guy doesn't believe in being "*friends*" with women, where's the relationship? That's what long lasting relationships are about. Someone that you can spend time with as well as your life. What's left after sex? You can't think clearly when your emotions are involved in decision making.

(6). **Guys think women come a dime a dozen. Prove them wrong! Don't cheat with him on his wife or girlfriend**. If a man commits to a woman for any length of time--he's usually committed. I've learned from others that even shacking is like being married. He can complain, but why's he still there if he isn't getting something he likes. Women need to be more of a sisterhood when it comes to handling "*heels*". Don't let him use you by having you and her. You'll more than likely come out the loser. I despise a whorish man! He's like a dog watching a tennis ball. He doesn't know which way to run.

(7). **You both need to have the same values and morals.** The KJB says, "*How can two walk together lest they agree.*" You need to see if he's going to walk the talk. Not just hand you a line to reel you in. You can't change anyone but yourself. If that person doesn't want nice things in life and doesn't want to save, there'll always be a battle. You have no business with a drug addict, alcoholic, smoking, cheating, disloyal person if you aren't the same kind of being. A god fearing church girl doesn't need a hell bent sinner. Your ambition and life styles should be alike. Friction will result if they aren't.

(8). **Know the type of guy you're attracted to and what types of guys are drawn to you**. Find out why this connection exists. Also pray for wisdom and discernment about relationships. For goodness sake, don't buy a guy gifts to show him you appreciate him. It should be the other way around. Your time is valuable. If he appreciates you, he should be pursuing you! Don't feel like you have to accept any old thing. It gets the relationship off on the wrong foot. How you start off with a guy, is what he'll expect. You will set the tone for the relationship. If he offers to do nice things for you, be wary of accepting too many favors, but expect him to be courteous and treat you well. If he offers to help you, don't have too much pride to let him shine. This is a fine line to walk. Don't take care of a man. Let him be a man and carry his own weight. If he's not going to help you, certainly don't allow him to take from you. This is a dishonorable thing and any honorable man wouldn't feel right doing that. You will not get your needs met if you insist upon being a doormat. Also, if you have to buy someone to hold onto them, what good are they to you, when crises arise in your life? You're really still alone, because that person won't support you when you need it.

(9). **Take dating seriously**. This is when teens **and** adults get into trouble. I really don't think young people should date before they turn 16 or 17 years old. Some adults shouldn't either. If and when dating is allowed by parents, then it should be supervised and chaperoned.

(10.) **Guys lie a lot. They think of it as a means to an end (the end being getting what they want by whatever means).** They know that if they really told you the truth, which is that they just wanted to use you for a season and drop you when someone better came along, would you accept it? Or they tell you that they wanted to take a joy ride at your expense. Some females do, accept this deal because they feel that no one really wants them (so they settle). Others accept the males because they mix truth with lies. A good example is a guy tells a woman or girl that she's pretty. If a girl knows that she is attractive (*because we do try to put our best foot forward*) that can be the truth--- but her looks and his intentions may have nothing to do with each other. So the girl feels that this is true and is flattered and thinks that this compliment comes from a good place. In reality, he is saying what he thinks and knows you want or need to hear (*the good stuff*). Anyone in their right mind wants to be admired and respected. Guys lie a lot and tell lots of half-truths for various reasons. Keep this in mind when dealing with males. Remember the fox!! What would any decent woman want for herself?

The Spider

The spider sits and spends its sticky bed.
It's threads are lies that a silver tongue has said.

The lines are all symmetrical, made up of our dreams.
When you get caught, you find that it wasn't quite what it
seemed.

As you slowly move towards your death—hope blinds you
cannot see. That the webs are light and strong—now you can't break
free.

You stepped into those lies, spun of gossamer threads,
Following your heart, not heeding those signs of dread.

For you it's too late to turn around.
After spider's finished, only empty shells are found.

He pricks you with his poison and takes away your strength.
He cares for nothing but his dangerous intent.

Had you listened to the warning in your head, you'd have had a
full life and would not his soul have fed.

Beware the spider, with venom in his kiss.
Heed wisdom when seeking love or your end will be like this.

The Beast

This beast called anger, rages within my chest.
Raging to be free, it will not let me rest.

The strides that I make to take me to the top, it topples
opportunities like a child's toy building blocks.

An errant word, meant to cause me hurt--Causes the beast,
itself to readily assert.

 Wisdom cries out, "Halt before it's too, too late!" All the great
plans
you've made, derailed by monstrous hate.

 The beast knows no reason, when it's ire is risen. It screams to
be free of it's .reasoning' prison.

"What did you say? You trying to make me look weak? I'll
show you, if it's strength that you seek!"

 You try to push it down, cause you know the damage it will do.
The rage inside hurts me, although directed toward you.

 I try to hold it in. I struggle to push it down. But it claws its way
up and out of my throat, it's bound!

"*Let me out! Set me free! I'll set all their wrongs to right.*" But I know within myself that these are lies. I never win these fights.

"*Help me, Help me! I don't want to be like this. A victim of emotions, a prisoner of these fits!*"

It's so strange, how this rage takes over and wins. It only abates, when it's ignited and then when it ends.

The bible says that, "*Anger rests in the bosom of a fool.*" It uses and abuses me. I'm left limp and weak, used up like a tool.

Many accolades and relations I have thrown away, because I can't stay this beast, and keep it at bay. I've lost jobs, hurt friends and close ones to my heart. Too late the damage is done and "***sorry***" is too small a remark.

The beast is satisfied, enjoying its meal, it snarls and roars with pride.
The beast relieved the pressure that felt like tons inside.

I don't want this animal, living within me, "*Take it all away, it's not who I want to be.*"

The wise man knows that this poison, must be bled out of the heart. Clip the claws and teeth of the beast or your life <u>will</u> be shorn apart.